foot + stool = footstool

Amanda Rondeau

Consulting Editor Monica Marx, M.A./Reading Specialist

ABDO
Publishing Company

Published by SandCastle™, an imprint of ABDO Publishing Company, 4940 Viking Drive, Edina, Minnesota 55435.

Printed in the United States.

Credits
Edited by: Pam Price
Curriculum Coordinator: Nancy Tuminelly
Cover and Interior Design and Production: Mighty Media
Photo Credits: Brand X Pictures, Comstock, Digital Vision, Eyewire Images, Hemera, ImageState, PhotoDisc

Library of Congress Cataloging-in-Publication Data

Rondeau, Amanda, 1974-
    Foot + stool = footstool / Amanda Rondeau.
      p. cm. -- (Compound words)
    Includes index.
    Summary: Illustrations and easy-to-read text introduce various compound words.
    ISBN 1-59197-433-X
      1. English language--Compound words--Juvenile literature. [1. English language--Compound words.] I. Title: Foot plus stool equals footstool. II. Title.
PE1175.R6657 2003
428.1--dc21
                                                                    2003048123

SandCastle™ books are created by a professional team of educators, reading specialists, and content developers around five essential components that include phonemic awareness, phonics, vocabulary, text comprehension, and fluency. All books are written, reviewed, and leveled for guided reading, early intervention reading, and Accelerated Reader® programs and designed for use in shared, guided, and independent reading and writing activities to support a balanced approach to literacy instruction.

Let Us Know

After reading the book, SandCastle would like you to tell us your stories about reading. What is your favorite page? Was there something hard that you needed help with? Share the ups and downs of learning to read. We want to hear from you! To get posted on the ABDO Publishing Company Web site, send us e-mail at:

sandcastle@abdopub.com

SandCastle Level: Transitional

A compound word is two words joined together to make a new word.

foot + stool =

footstool

Leah and Maya lean on the footstool.

key + hole =

keyhole

Becky put the key in the keyhole to open the door.

door + way =

doorway

Jenny's mom leaves early for work.

She kisses Jenny good-bye in the doorway.

up + stairs =

upstairs

Our school's front door is upstairs from the sidewalk.

news + paper =

newspaper

Fred's aunt likes to read the newspaper on the front porch.

home + work =

homework

Dan does his homework in his bedroom after school.

Ida's Big Adventure

Our cat Ida found
a moth inside.

She chased it into
the bedroom,
where it tried
to hide.

The moth flew past Ida and
down the staircase.

It hid on a footstool behind a
large suitcase.

The moth flew to the door and
out the keyhole!

Maybe Ida should try chasing
a mole!

More Compound Words

archway	household
armchair	housework
bathroom	outlet
bathtub	pincushion
bedspread	rooftop
bookshelf	stairway
dishwasher	stovetop
downstairs	wallpaper
fireplace	washcloth

Glossary

bedroom   a room where someone sleeps

footstool   a low stool to rest your feet on

keyhole   the slot in a lock that a key fits into

porch   a covered room at the entrance to a building

staircase   a flight of steps that connects different levels in a building

upstairs   on a higher floor

About SandCastle™

A professional team of educators, reading specialists, and content developers created the SandCastle™ series to support young readers as they develop reading skills and strategies and increase their general knowledge. The SandCastle™ series has four levels that correspond to early literacy development in young children. The levels are provided to help teachers and parents select the appropriate books for young readers.

Emerging Readers
(no flags)

Beginning Readers
(1 flag)

Transitional Readers
(2 flags)

Fluent Readers
(3 flags)

These levels are meant only as a guide. All levels are subject to change.

To see a complete list of SandCastle™ books and other nonfiction titles from ABDO Publishing Company, visit **www.abdopub.com** or contact us at:

4940 Viking Drive, Edina, Minnesota 55435 • 1-800-800-1312 • fax: 1-952-831-1632